To Wilder, Laken, and North.
Thanks for finding
wild cheetahs with me!

— Aunt Kate

For my kind, loving,
and brilliant mom.

— Ash

CHEETAHS RETURN TO INDIA

The True Story of Aasha and Pavan

By KATE RIETEMA
Art by ASH ROY

TILBURY HOUSE PUBLISHERS

Long ago, Asiatic cheetahs sprinted across India's grasslands,

roamed through open forests,

and snoozed in the shade of khair trees.

But grassland turned into villages, food disappeared, and people hunted cheetahs for profit and sport.

Then . . . five.

Four.

Three.

Two.

One.

Zero.

A swirl of wind erased their final pawprints,
and they were gone.

For seventy years, India missed her beloved cheetahs.

Then one day, blades whirred overhead. Two helicopters landed in Kuno National Park, bringing a brave delivery from Namibia.

Eight African cheetahs. Could these cheetahs make a new home in India?

At first, the cheetahs explored their new home from the safety of a spacious enclosure.

The cheetahs played, hunted, and napped. They proved they were healthy, strong, and ready for the wild.

Two cheetahs would be chosen
as the first to sprint free . . .

but who?

Aasha and Pavan.

Aasha was a confident female.
Her name was special
—it meant *hope*.

Pavan was an adventurous male. His name matched his speed —it meant *wind*.

they raced like wind into the wild,
leaving pawprints across India.

On his first night, Pavan snoozed in the shelter of a khair tree.

On her first morning, Aasha woke to the song of weaverbirds.

But they had lived in the enclosure for many months— were they still fast enough to catch prey in the unfenced wild?

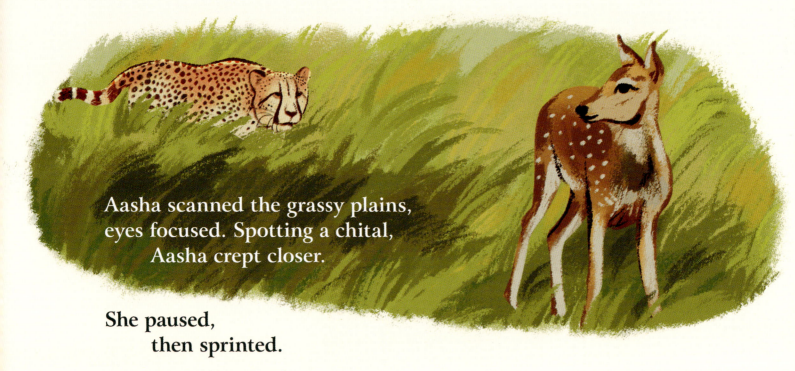

Aasha scanned the grassy plains, eyes focused. Spotting a chital, Aasha crept closer.

She paused,
 then sprinted.

She was still fast—over 70 miles per hour.
 But her prey escaped.

She tried again.

Aasha waited, muscles tense.
Then, in a flash, she raced after a blackbuck—her claws gripping the earth, pushing her even faster.

Again, she missed her target.
Aasha was growing tired.

Days turned into weeks,
and more cheetahs were released.

The Indian sun spilled heat across Kuno National Park. Temperatures climbed higher than anything the cheetahs had known in Namibia. 95 degrees. 100 degrees. 116 degrees. The heat was too brutal for some of the other cheetahs.

But Aasha and Pavan survived.

Then came rain.
The Indian sky spilled
water for days and days.
No hiding place was dry.

The wetness soaked through
Pavan's thick scruff.
His skin itched.

He scratched with muddy claws, and infection spread like fire.
Flies swarmed over the wounds around Pavan's neck. The humidity
was too harsh and infections too deep for some of the other cheetahs.

But Aasha and Pavan survived.

A cool breeze quieted the heat,
and the rain slowed to a drip.

Then one day,
the grass rustled. What was it?

Cubs!
One.   Two.   Three!

Three cheetah cubs
pounced and tumbled.

They snoozed in the shelter of khair trees,
and woke to the song of weaverbirds.

And what about tomorrow?
Will their numbers grow
to reach a hundred?
And then a thousand?

We don't know yet.

But for now, Aasha, Pavan, and the cubs are leaving pawprints across India.

Author's Note

In the early 1900's, 100,000 cheetahs roamed freely throughout Africa, the Middle East, and parts of Asia. Sadly, this number has dropped to less than 7,000 cheetahs today. Cheetahs are nearing extinction in the Middle East, and prior to Project Cheetah, they had been extinct in India for seventy years.

Pavan — Photo Credit: @Eli.H.Walker / CCF

Project Cheetah is a collaborative effort to reestablish a population of cheetahs in India. Kuno National Park was chosen as the first site for the cheetahs' translocation because of its abundant prey and grasslands. In 2022, the first eight cheetahs were flown from Namibia to India and placed into quarantine enclosures. After a period of observation, the cheetahs were transferred to bomas—larger, fenced sections of the park. The first two cheetahs, Aasha and Pavan, were finally released into India's wild in 2023. To maintain a viable population of cheetahs, India signed an agreement with South Africa to translocate an additional twelve cheetahs annually for the next eight to ten years.

Since the cheetahs' arrival in India, Project Cheetah has experienced both celebrations and setbacks. We cheered the birth of new cubs, and grieved as other cheetahs died due to infection, dehydration, and natural causes. Since the writing of this book, we learned the difficult news of Pavan's death due to drowning.

During my recent visit to Namibia, I discussed these difficulties with Lea Petersen, the head cheetah keeper at the Cheetah Conservation Fund. I asked Lea what she wanted readers to remember, and Lea said, "Even if our work is really tough, and even if we don't get the results we hoped for, we still need to try."

Aasha — Photo Credit: @Eli.H.Walker / CCF

Together, we remain hopeful that this bold step in conservation is just the beginning of many cheetah generations yet to come.

Timeline of Important Events

- **1952**
  Cheetahs officially declared extinct in India

- **2009**
  Project Cheetah begins, setting the goal to re-establish a population of cheetahs in India

- **2020**
  Project Cheetah is approved by India's Supreme Court

- **September 17, 2022**
  Eight cheetahs arrive in India from Namibia and are released into bomas

- **February 18, 2023**
  Twelve additional cheetahs arrive from South Africa

- **March 11, 2023**
  Aasha & Pavan are the first cheetahs released into the wild

- **July 14, 2023**
  Pavan is captured, returned to a boma, and treated for infection

- **July 20, 2023**
  Aasha is captured, returned to a boma, and treated for infection

- **December 21, 2023**
  Pavan is released back into the wild

- **December 26, 2023**
  Three cubs are born to Aasha

- **August 27, 2024**
  Pavan's death

- **February 5, 2025**
  Aasha and cubs are released into the wild

Special Thanks

Special thanks to Dr. Laurie Marker, Lea Petersen, Eli Walker, and all the staff at the Cheetah Conservation Fund for offering their expertise and hospitality during the creation of this book. Your commitment to cheetah conservation is an inspiration to many.

Thank you.

Cheetah Conservation Fund

The Cheetah Conservation Fund (CCF) is a world-renowned research and educational organization in Namibia, Africa, whose mission is the conservation of cheetahs and their ecosystems. CCF played a vital role in bringing cheetahs back to India.

> "To save cheetahs from extinction, we need to create permanent places for them on Earth. The cheetah needs massive amounts of support to survive, and it is my hope that we, as conservationists, can provide what the species requires for success."

—Dr. Laurie Marker
CCF's Founder and Executive Director

Text Copyright © 2025 Kate Rietema
Illustration Copyright © 2025 Ash Roy
Design Copyright © 2024 Tilbury House Publishers
Hardcover ISBN: 9781668955192

Library of Congress Cataloging-in-Publication Data has been filed.
LC record available at https://lccn.loc.gov/2025008524

Publisher expressly prohibits the use of this work in connection with
the development of any software program, including, without limitation,
training a machine learning or generative artificial intelligence (AI)system.

All rights reserved. No part of this book may be reproduced in
any manner without the express written consent of the publisher,
except in the case of brief excerpts in critical reviews and articles.
All inquiries should be addressed to:

an imprint of
Cherry Lake Publishing Group
2395 South Huron Parkway, Suite 200
Ann Arbor, Michigan 48104
www.tilburyhouse.com

Printed in China

10 9 8 7 6 5 4 3 2 1